DATE DUE

	DATE DUE		

The Universe

Galaxies

Anne Welsbacher

ABDO & Daughters

Published by Abdo & Daughters, 4940 Viking Drive, Suite 622, Edina, Minnesota 55435.

Copyright © 1997 by Abdo Consulting Group, Inc., Pentagon Tower, P.O. Box 36036, Minneapolis, Minnesota 55435 USA. International copyrights reserved in all countries. No part of this book may be reproduced in any form without written permission from the publisher.

Printed in the United States.

Cover and Interior Photo credits: Peter Arnold, Inc.
Wide World Photos

Illustrations: Ben Dann Lander
Edited by Bob Italia

Library of Congress Cataloging-in-Publication Data

Welsbacher, Anne, 1955-
Galaxies / Anne Welsbacher.
    p. cm. — (The universe)
Includes index.
Summary: Presents a brief discussion of the properties of galaxies, including the Milky Way and others.
ISBN 1-56239-719-2
1. Galaxies—Juvenile literature. [1. Galaxies.] I. Title. II. Series: Welsbacher, Anne, 1955- Universe.
QB857.3.W45 1997
523.1'12—dc20   96-9190
                                                         CIP
                                                         AC

ABOUT THE AUTHOR
Anne Welsbacher is the director of publications for the Science Museum of Minnesota. She has written and edited science books and articles for children, and has written for national and regional publications on science, the environment, the arts, and other topics.

Revised Edition 2002

Contents

Galaxies

Our Sun is one of trillions of stars in space. Stars group together into clusters. These **star clusters** form bigger groups called **galaxies**.

There are three main kinds of galaxies: **elliptical**, **spiral**, and **irregular**. All are made of stars. Some also contain gas and dust. Galaxies are held together by **gravity**, a force that draws all things toward each galaxy's center.

Galaxies cluster together, too. These clusters can band together into **superclusters** of galaxies!

elliptical   **spiral**   **irregular**

The Andromeda galaxy.

Elliptical Galaxies

Elliptical galaxies are round or elliptical shaped. An elliptical shape is a circle that has been stretched wider in the middle.

An elliptical galaxy contains little or no gas and dust. Its stars are old and not as bright as young stars.

Stars in elliptical galaxies move in all directions. Many elliptical galaxies are small compared to other kinds of galaxies.

Opposite page: Hubble Space Telescope image of the giant elliptical galaxy called NGC 1275.

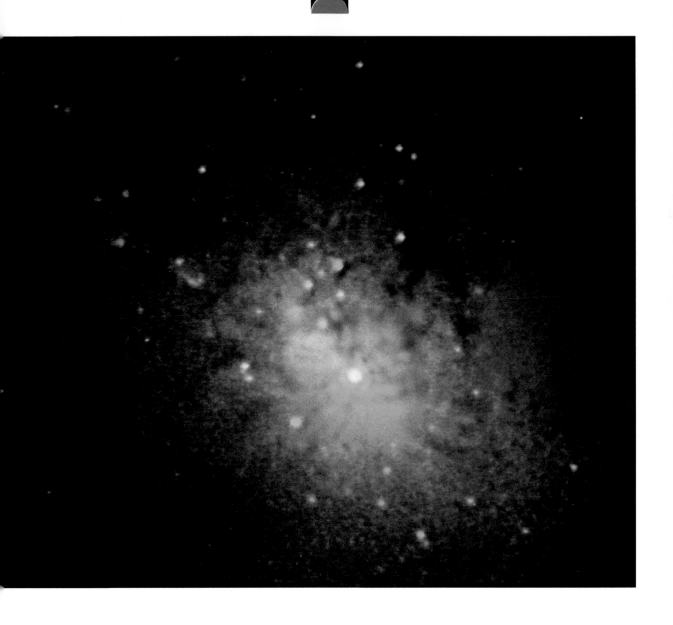

Spiral Galaxies

About half of all galaxies are **spiral galaxies**—including the Earth's galaxy, the Milky Way.

Spiral galaxies are shaped like a pinwheel. Their spiral "arms" of stars come out from their centers. Some spirals are tight and bright. Others are looser, with more distance between each star.

Ordinary spiral galaxies have an S-shaped center. Barred spiral galaxies look like they have a bar through the center.

Spiral galaxies contain stars, gas, and dust. New stars form in their spirals. Most of the stars rotate around the galaxies' centers.

A spiral galaxy.

Irregular Galaxies

Irregular galaxies are the most common type of galaxy. They have no special shape. Something may have upset their shape, or their stars might not have enough movement to form a shape.

Irregular galaxies have lots of dust and gas which will one day turn into stars. Most irregular galaxies do not shine brightly.

Opposite page: The Hubble Space Telescope image of the galaxy called NGC 7252 reveals a "mini-spiral" disk of gas, dust, and stars.

Other Galaxies

There are other, less common, types of **galaxies**. The huge cD galaxies are elliptical shaped and filled with tight **star clusters**.

Dwarf galaxies can be elliptical or irregular shaped. They may have many or few clusters.

"Ghost" galaxies do not give off much light. They look like the ghosts of **spiral galaxies**.

Opposite page: A large, faint "ghost" galaxy.

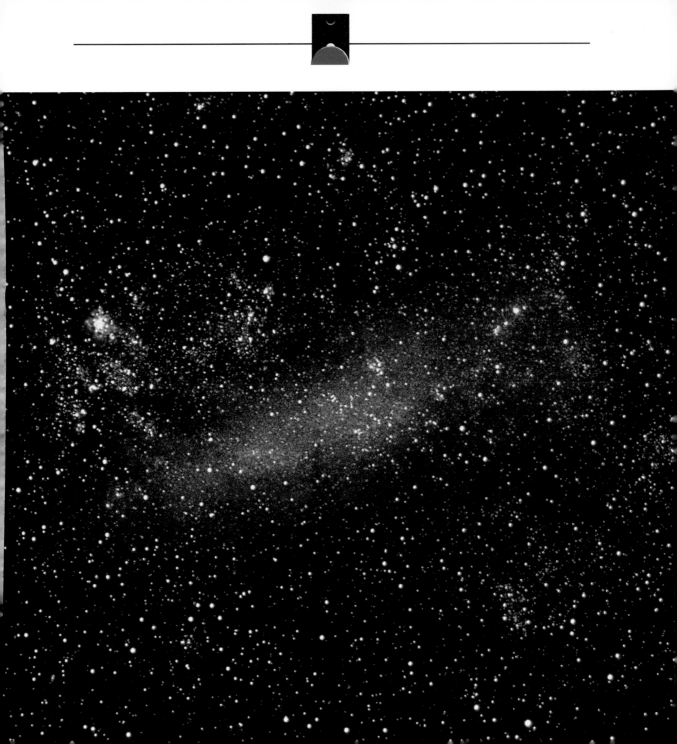

Star Clusters

All **galaxies** have **star clusters**. Open star clusters have 25 to 1,000 stars, and lots of gas and dust. The stars are loosely grouped. Our Sun and **Solar System** are in an open star cluster.

Globular clusters have thousands or millions of stars. They are grouped much closer together and give off much light.

Opposite page: This ultraviolet image taken by Astro-I on the Space Shuttle Columbia is of the young star cluster 30 Doradus. It is located 170,000 light-years from Earth.

The Milky Way

The Earth's **galaxy**—the Milky Way—is a giant **spiral galaxy**. The Milky Way has over 100 billion stars, and more than 1,000 open **star clusters**. Our nearest neighbor in the Milky Way is a star system called Alpha and Proxima Centauri.

The Sun and **Solar System** are between the center and edge of the Milky Way galaxy. The Sun **orbits** the center of the galaxy, just as the planets orbit the Sun. It takes the Sun 240 million years to make one orbit around the Milky Way.

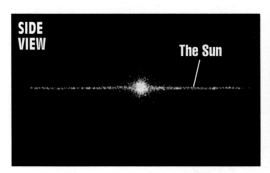
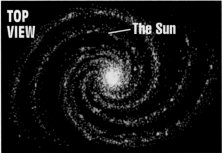

The Milky Way galaxy.

The center of the Milky Way galaxy viewed from Earth.

Galaxy Clusters

Galaxies group together into **galaxy clusters**. The Milky Way is one of 17 galaxies in a cluster called the Local Group.

Other galaxies in the Local Group are the Andromeda galaxy and the two Magellanic Clouds. They are the three galaxies closest to the Milky Way. Andromeda is a **spiral galaxy** much like the Milky Way. The Magellanic Clouds are **irregular galaxies**.

The galaxy cluster closest to the Local Group is called Virgo. Virgo has hundreds of galaxies. The Local Group is moving slowly toward Virgo.

Opposite page: This star field consists of the Andromeda galaxy and the Magellanic Clouds.

Galaxies and the Universe

Galaxies and their clusters are part of the Universe. The Universe is all of space. Many scientists believe it formed about 15 billion years ago by a giant explosion called the **Big Bang**.

Galaxies are still growing and pulling together. And they continue to move slowly through space.

Scientists name most galaxies with numbers. But a few galaxies have word names. The Milky Way is one such galaxy. Others are called Whirlpool, Antennae, Pinwheel, and Cartwheel.

Opposite page: The Whirlpool Galaxy.

Galaxy Facts

The Milky Way
- •Size ---------------------------------- 100,000 light-years* across
- •Type ---------------------------------- spiral
- •Number of stars ------------------- 100 billion
- •Closest star system
    to the Solar System ------------- Alpha and Proxima Centauri
                                        (4.3 light-years away)

- •Closest galaxy ---------------------- The Large Magellanic Cloud
                                        (150,000 light-years away)

Size of Local Group cluster -------- 17 galaxies, including
                                        the Milky Way

Closest cluster ----------------------- Virgo (50-60 million
                                        light-years away)

Number of galaxies in Universe --- billions

*a light-year equals the distance it takes light to travel through space in one year (over 5 trillion miles [8 trillion km]).

Glossary

Big Bang—a giant explosion that happened in space 15 billion years ago. Many scientists believe the Universe was formed by the Big Bang.

elliptical (e-LIP-tuh-kull) **galaxy**—a round-shaped galaxy.

galaxy—a large group of stars, and sometimes gas and dust, held together by gravity.

galaxy cluster—a group of galaxies banded together.

gravity—a force that draws all things toward their center.

irregular (ear-REG-yoo-ler) **galaxy**—one kind of galaxy that has no special shape.

orbit—The path of any heavenly body about another heavenly body.

Solar System—Our Sun and all the things that orbit it, including the Earth, the Moon, and all the other planets.

spiral galaxy—a pinwheel-shaped galaxy.

star cluster—a group of stars within a galaxy.

supercluster—galaxy clusters grouped together.

Index